P9-ELR-902

j921
WILLIAM

Hilliam, Paul.

William the
Conqueror.

$31.95

DATE			

BAKER & TAYLOR

LEADERS OF THE
MIDDLE AGES™

WILLIAM THE
CONQUEROR

First Norman
King of England

LEADERS OF THE MIDDLE AGES™

WILLIAM THE CONQUEROR

First Norman King of England

Paul Hilliam

The Rosen Publishing Group, Inc., New York

Dedicated to Jonathan Hilliam

Published in 2005 by The Rosen Publishing Group, Inc.
29 East 21st Street, New York, NY 10010

First Edition

Library of Congress Cataloging-in-Publication Data

Hilliam, Paul.
William the Conqueror: first Norman king of England / Paul Hilliam. — 1st ed.
    p. cm. — (Leaders of the Middle Ages)
Includes bibliographical references and index.
ISBN 1-4042-0166-1 (lib. bdg.)
1. William I, King of England, 1027 or 8–1087. 2. Great Britain—History—William I, 1066–1087. 3. Great Britain—Kings and rulers—Biography. 4. Nobility—France—Normandy—Biography. 5. Normandy (France)—History—To 1515. 6. Normans—Great Britain—Biography.
I. Title. II. Series.
DA197.H48 2004
942.02'1'092—dc22

                                                            2004003426

Manufactured in the United States of America

On the cover: Background: Late eleventh-century depiction of the Norman Conquest of England as seen on the Bayeux Tapestry. Inset: Thirteenth-century English miniature (portrait) of William the Conqueror.

CONTENTS

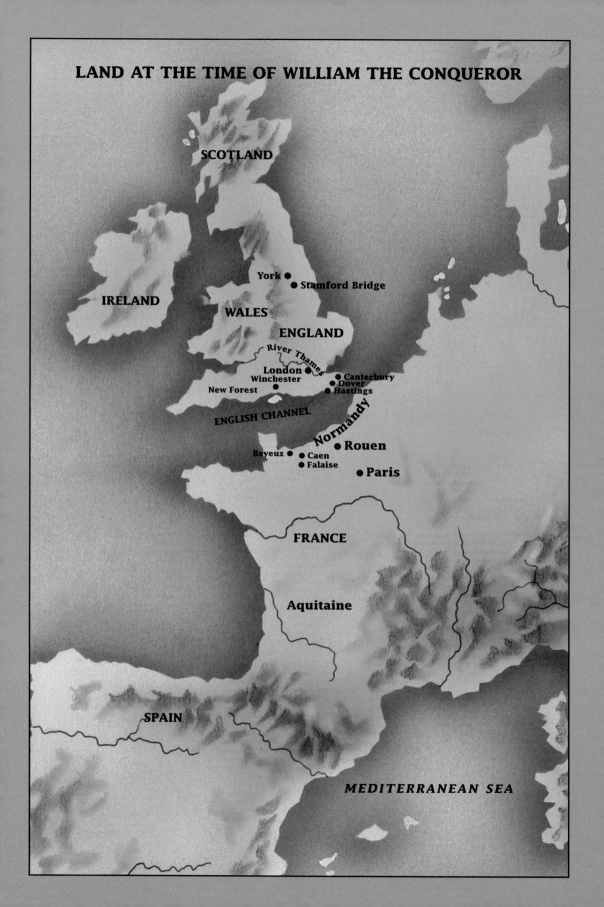

LAND AT THE TIME OF WILLIAM THE CONQUEROR

SCOTLAND

IRELAND

York ●
● Stamford Bridge

WALES

ENGLAND

River Thames

London ●
Winchester ●
New Forest

● Canterbury
● Dover
● Hastings

ENGLISH CHANNEL

Normandy

● Rouen

Bayeux ●
● Caen
● Falaise

● Paris

FRANCE

Aquitaine

SPAIN

MEDITERRANEAN SEA

INTRODUCTION: THE BAYEUX TAPESTRY

The year 1066 is perhaps the most well-known date in English history. It was the year in which William, Duke of Normandy (an area of northern France), invaded England and defeated King Harold at the Battle of Hastings. He then became King William I of England.

During his life, William gained great power, wealth, and influence. Later in history, he became known as the Conqueror. However, William did more than merely conquer England.

His actions as king and the way in which he ruled changed and shaped the course of English history. Under the guidance of King William, the country was governed in a different way. New laws were made and castles were built. Even the English language changed dramatically when it began to incorporate the French spoken by the Norman invaders.

The Battle of Hastings, on October 14, 1066, was the first phase of the conquest of England by Duke William of Normandy. In this scene from the Bayeux Tapestry, Norman knights on horseback are shown charging at the Saxons, who fought on foot. After William's victory at Hastings, the remaining Saxon earls realized the hopelessness of their position, and William was crowned king of England on Christmas Day, 1066.

The story of William the Conqueror is also interesting because of the number of accounts of his life that have survived. People at the time realized how important a man William was and how significant his achievements were. Because of this, they recorded his life for future generations. The most interesting

source of information, by far, is the Bayeux Tapestry. This is a very long piece of linen cloth, measuring 230 feet (70 meters) in length and 20 inches (51 centimeters) in width.

The tapestry can be seen in a museum in Bayeux, a beautiful small town in Normandy. It is rather like a cartoon strip because it has a script written on it (though it's in Latin), as well as very skillfully produced artwork. Embroidered on the cloth are pictures telling the story of the events leading up to and including the invasion of England and the Battle of Hastings.

The story told in the Bayeux Tapestry stops with the Battle of Hastings. Unfortunately, however, historians think there is a section of the cloth that is missing from the end. It is possible that this missing piece showed William's coronation in London. Nevertheless, what is certain is that the tapestry tells the story from a Norman point of view.

HISTORICAL SOURCES

Quite a number of historical sources give information about William and his invasion of England. By comparing all these sources, it is possible to get a clear sense of what may have happened during 1066.

Although the Bayeux Tapestry is the most important source, English sources include *The Anglo-Saxon Chronicle* (a yearly account of events in England, kept by English monks) and books by two Saxon monks named Florence of Worcester and William of Malmesbury.

Norman sources include a book entitled *Gesta Guillelmi Ducis Normannorum* (The Deeds of William Duke of the Normans), written by William of Poitiers (who was one of William the Conqueror's soldiers before becoming a monk); a book entitled *Gesta Normannorum Ducis* (The Deeds of the Duke of the Normans), written between 1070 and 1072 by a monk named William of Jumièges; and a book entitled the *Ecclesiastical History of England and Normandy*, written by another monk named Ordericus Vitalis, who lived during the twelfth century.

The Bayeux Tapestry was commissioned by William's half brother, Bishop Odo. Although it was probably made in Kent, England, Odo intended it to hang in his cathedral in Bayeux. Bishop Odo actually fought alongside William at Hastings. He obviously thought that he played an important part in the Norman invasion of England, as he is shown on the tapestry more often than anybody else!

The character of William becomes evident through the events of his life. He was a strong, determined, energetic man, who was prepared to be ruthless to achieve his goals. Yet he was also admired by many people during his life as a just ruler, who was tolerant of those who kept the law. He was certainly a man of vision and a charismatic leader.

WILLIAM, DUKE OF NORMANDY

CHAPTER 1

For about 300 years, from the late eighth century onward, groups of fierce Vikings from Norway, Sweden, and Denmark raided the coasts of Europe. They were skilled sailors who navigated the open seas in long wooden boats. These were powered by sails when there was wind and by oars when it was calm. Wherever the Vikings landed, they attacked local people and stole valuables from towns and villages. Everyone from peasants to monks in monasteries fled for their lives from the people they called Northmen, or Norsemen.

THE NORMANS

In the early tenth century, one group of Norsemen from Norway—led by a man called Rolf (sometimes called Rollo)—sailed its boats up the river

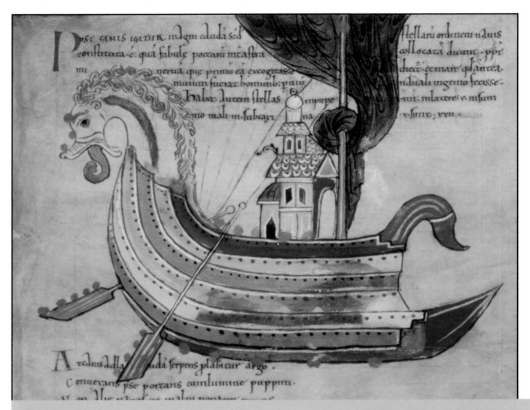

Above is an Anglo-Saxon manuscript page showing a Viking longboat. The boats that the Normans used were similar in design. They had a single sail attached to a mast, and they could also be rowed. The shallow draught on these boats meant that they could navigate rivers. The smaller longboats were light enough to be carried overground by their crew. Their design made them strong enough to withstand stormy conditions at sea.

Seine in France and captured the city of Rouen. Charles III, the king of the French, or Franks as they were then known, realized that he was powerless to remove these invaders. In 911, Charles III granted Rolf rule over the area he controlled. This area became known as Normandy (now part of northwest France). The Norsemen who settled there were soon referred to as Normans.

EVIDENCE OF THE NORMANS' VIKING ROOTS

A stone carved in runic characters (early Viking writing) was found in the yard of the St. Ouen Church in Rouen, France. Stones carved with runic characters are found mainly in Scandinavia, hence the stone in Rouen is evidence of the Normans' Viking roots. Over the years, however, the Normans gradually mixed with the local population and adopted the French language. They also converted to Christianity.

The Norsemen had an alphabet consisting of sixteen letters known as runes. Inscriptions were written on bone, wood, and stone for a number of reasons, such as to declare ownership of land or to commemorate the dead. The letters were composed mostly of straight lines, which made them easier to carve.

Rolf and his two successors took the title of count, but the next ruler, Richard I (William's great-grandfather), took the title Duke of Normandy. Richard was a man of power and influence. His sister, Emma, was married to Ethelred, a Saxon king of England, and this later turned out to be a factor in William's claim to the English throne. Nevertheless, Richard regarded the king of France as his superior overlord.

WILLIAM'S BIRTH AND CHILDHOOD

Duke Robert I of Normandy was about seventeen years old when his son, William, was born in either late 1027 or early 1028. An exact record was not kept, possibly because the birth was illegitimate.

From his castle walls in the Norman town of Falaise, Robert had seen a good-looking girl about his age, who was washing her clothes in the valley below. Her name was Herlève (although she was also known as Arlette). She was the daughter of the local leather tanner. Robert was unable to resist her, and as a result of their relationship, Herlève later gave birth to William and his sister, Adelaide.

However, at this time, Robert was engaged to a sister of King Canute of Denmark, and Herlève was

later married off to another noble. It was obvious to all that William and his sister had been born outside marriage. As a result, for many years, William was angered by the nickname that he was given, William the Bastard.

In 1034, Duke Robert decided that he was going to Jerusalem on a pilgrimage. He summoned his uncle, Robert, archbishop of Rouen, and his nobles, and he asked them to recognize William as the next duke. The following year, when Robert died on the return journey from the Holy Land, William became the next duke. At the time, he was only seven years old.

During the Middle Ages, people undertook journeys—known as pilgrimages—to visit places associated with the lives of saints. The relics of saints (either parts of their bodies or objects that had belonged to them) were kept in special containers known as reliquaries and housed in churches and cathedrals. The tomb of an important saint or a significant relic would attract large numbers of pilgrims hoping that the saint would answer their prayers.

William's great-uncle, Archbishop Robert, looked after William and his land in Normandy. Henry I of France also supported William's claim to be duke. However, when Archbishop Robert died in 1037, various Norman nobles who were hungry for power started to threaten William's life. On one occasion, during an attempt to assassinate William, a servant was killed in the room where the young boy was sleeping. Later, two of his guardian nobles, Count Alan of Brittany and Count Gilbert of Brionne, were murdered. Another story tells of an occasion in which, fearing for his life, William had to gallop on his horse to his castle in Falaise while being chased. He was growing up fast, and he was quickly learning how to take care of himself.

WILLIAM, DUKE OF NORMANDY

In 1047, around the age of twenty, William faced a serious rebellion. A group of nobles in western Normandy supported William's cousin, Guy of Burgundy. He claimed to have a more acceptable reason and right to rule the area. He stated he was a direct descendant of the earlier dukes.

On this occasion, the French king, Henry I, came to aid William. The young duke showed his growing military skill as he defeated the rebel army at Val-és-Dunes near Caen on the north coast of Normandy. Later that year, William showed his skills as a ruler and lawmaker when he presided over a church council that imposed what became known as the Treaty of God. This treaty banned private wars between Wednesday evenings and Monday mornings, as well as during religious festivals.

The ruling did not apply to William and the king of France. However, anyone else who broke it was to be excommunicated by the church. This was serious punishment in those days, since people believed that being banned from the church meant that a person would go to hell rather than heaven.

William hoped that the Treaty of God would allow him to control his nobles, but he continued to feel threatened, both from within Normandy and from beyond its borders. Guy of Burgundy, who was wounded at the battle of Val-és-Dunes, defied William from within the walls of his castle at Brionne during a siege that lasted three years.

A more serious threat to William was posed by Geoffrey Martel, Count of Anjou and Maine. Martel captured castles at Domfront and Alençon, just south of Normandy. To secure his borders, William attacked both castles. He was unsuccessful at

Domfront, but at Alençon, he was so enraged when he was made fun of for being a "tanner" that when he captured the castle, he burnt it down and cut off the limbs of all those who had made fun of him. Terrified, the people of Domfront quickly surrendered. From then on, William's authority as a military leader was unquestioned.

MARRIAGE

William was about twenty when he set out to marry Matilda, the daughter of Count Baldwin V of Flanders (an area roughly equivalent to present-day Belgium). Through this arranged marriage (negotiated with Matilda's father), William hoped to secure an ally on the eastern borders of his dukedom. But Matilda was a headstrong teenager. At first, she refused the proposal. It is said that William rode to her father's home in Lille, pulled the girl's braided hair, and kicked her around her room. Then he left her to rethink his proposal.

Eventually, Matilda was attracted to William's fiery character and finally agreed to marry him. However, in 1049, Pope Leo IX forbade the marriage because William and Matilda might have been cousins. However, it is an indication of William's determination and defiant personality that despite this obstacle, he went ahead with the marriage in 1053. As a consequence, both the duke and his young duchess were excommunicated.

This was the worst punishment a pope could pronounce. However, although it would certainly have weighed heavily upon William's conscience, in practice it changed little. It was not until 1059 that the excommunication was lifted. And this was following an appeal to the pope made by William's friend Lanfranc. Lanfranc was a prior of the abbey at Bec. As a penance, William and Matilda were then required to start two abbeys in Caen. These were St. Étienne, the Abbaye-aux-hommes for monks, and La Trinité, the Abbaye-aux-dames for nuns. La Trinité can still be seen in Caen. William and Matilda were later buried in the abbeys they founded. In recognition for his part in obtaining papal approval for the marriage, Lanfranc eventually became archbishop of Canterbury.

Although they did not marry for love, there was certainly growing affection between the young couple. They must have looked rather odd together. William was tall and would later become quite large, whereas Matilda was very small. Excavation of her grave in 1961 suggested that she was 4 feet 2 inches (1.3 meters) tall. Between them, they would eventually have four sons and five daughters.

Lanfranc of Pavia, prior of Bec, was appointed as head of the Abbaye-aux-hommes when it was founded. He remained head until 1070 when he was appointed archbishop of Canterbury. The facade of the church of St. Étienne (part of the abbey) was the first example of such a harmonious Norman facade. Its architecture inspired many of the great French cathedrals that were built in the following century.

Matilda was a constant support to her husband. And in what was considered unusual behavior for those days, it is believed that William remained a loyal husband. It may well have been his illegitimate background that led William to be a faithful husband. He knew firsthand what it meant to be born outside marriage. Also, he may have wanted to avoid any difficulties that could be caused by illegitimate children claiming a right to inherit land and power after his death.

William's marriage brought about a further period of instability for Normandy. King Henry I of France, who was still William's overlord, was worried about the duke's growing influence. To contain his power, Henry formed an alliance with Geoffrey Martel, Count of Anjou and Maine, who was William's former enemy south of Normandy. They would help each other if William tried to expand the area he ruled.

At about the same time, within Normandy, the Count of Talou declared that he opposed William's claim to be duke. He proclaimed his right to the dukedom. The Count of Talou was William's uncle and the son of William's grandfather Duke Richard II by his second marriage. The count had not supported William at the battle at Domfront and he built himself a strongly fortified castle at Arques in eastern Normandy, which bordered land ruled by Henry I. From there, the count hoped that, in time, he would be able to attack his illegitimate nephew.

William laid siege to Arques, and the Count of Talou was forced to leave Normandy. Later, William successfully defeated King Henry I's two attempts to invade his lands. This happened once in 1054 at the Battle of Mortemer in eastern Normandy and then in 1056 when Henry joined forces with Count Geoffrey Martel to attack William from the south. From then on, William's rule was secure, but during these earlier battles, William and his Norman knights gained the military experience that later enabled them to invade England.

THE BACKGROUND TO THE NORMAN INVASION OF ENGLAND

When King Edward of England died in January 1066, there was a crisis. Edward the Confessor, as he was known, did not have any children, and there was no close blood relative to become the next king or queen. Edward's brother-in-law, Harold Godwineson, Earl of Wessex, became king. However, there were several people, including Duke William of Normandy, who thought that they should be the next ruler instead. The situation was complicated. The roots of the problem stretched back into English history.

FROM THE DARK AGES TO SAXON ENGLAND

The term "Dark Ages" is used by historians to describe the period in British history following the year 410, when England was no longer part of the

Roman Empire. It is a period about which relatively little is known. In fact, one might say we are "in the dark" about what happened at this time, as few records were kept. When the Romans retreated to Italy in order to defend their homeland against barbarian attacks, Britannia (modern-day England) was left vulnerable to raiders from Denmark and Germany. Angles (where the name England comes from) and Saxons were some of the people who journeyed across the North Sea. They were eager to find good farmland and a mild climate in which to settle.

By the year 600, there were about a dozen small kingdoms in England. And with the spread of Christianity from mainland Europe, churches and monasteries soon began to appear. Historical records were kept by monks, most notably Bede, a Northumbrian monk, who completed a book called *History of the English Church and People* in 731.

On their raids, Vikings would often find many metal coins and objects. This treasure would be very useful for them in terms of providing them with means of trading with foreigners.

This is an image of Canute the Great (995–1035) *(bottom right)*, king of Denmark from 1018 to 1035, and Queen Elfgiva *(bottom left)*. Canute was also the king of England from 1016 to 1035 and the king of Norway from 1028 to 1035.

During his reign (871–899), King Alfred the Great of Wessex (a large area of central southern England) emerged as the strongest of the Saxon kings. Under his leadership, Viking raiders from Scandinavia suffered a series of defeats. Their settlements were restricted to eastern and northern England. (Around the same time, Rolf, William's Viking ancestor, settled in northern France.)

One of Alfred's achievements was initiating *The Anglo-Saxon Chronicle*. This was an account of events in England that monks were expected to keep. At this time, a more sophisticated society was starting to emerge from the Dark Ages. Alfred's son and grandson managed to unite much of England, but then the Viking raids started again.

King Ethelred II of England tried to bribe the Vikings to leave his kingdom alone, but the Vikings returned, demanding more money. Finally, Canute (sometimes spelled "Cnut"), brother of the king of Denmark, captured the whole of England and became king from 1016 until his death in 1035. For a short time, Canute also ruled Sweden and Norway.

At this point, it seemed that England was destined to be part of a great Scandinavian empire. However, both of Canute's sons died soon after their father. With no obvious successor to follow Canute, the vast empire over which he ruled fell apart. Next, Edward (Ethelred's son) became king. However, he died without producing an heir. The question of who next should be king of England gave William, Duke of Normandy, his chance to claim the throne.

HAROLD SUCCEEDS EDWARD AS KING OF ENGLAND

In Britain today, the eldest son of the monarch is next in line to the throne. If there is no son, then the oldest daughter becomes queen. Whatever the case,

KING EDWARD THE CONFESSOR

Edward I, the Saxon who ruled from 1043 to 1066, was the son of Ethelred and Emma of Normandy. When Ethelred died in 1016, Emma married King Canute. She sent Edward to Normandy for his own safety.

When Edward returned as king, he was regarded as being more French than English, and the Norman advisers he brought with him annoyed the English nobles.

Edward was nicknamed "the Confessor" because he was regarded as being more like a priest than a strong monarch. Toward the end of his life, he was very occupied with the building of Westminster Abbey. This became the most important church in London. Built near the river Thames, it is the place where many English kings and queens were buried. It is believed that as a young man, Edward took a vow of chastity. This meant that he failed to produce a child who might succeed him, even though he was married to Edith, daughter of Harold Godwineson, Earl of Wessex.

This detail from the Bayeux Tapestry shows Edward the Confessor and Harold. Edward, the Anglo-Saxon king, sent Harold as a messenger to Duke William of Normandy. This image suggests that Harold was to pronounce William the next in line to the throne of England.

a definite order of who should become the next monarch is well established. But a blood relationship in Saxon England was just one factor to take into consideration—although this was a very important one. It was also vital that whoever ruled the country commanded the loyalty of the nobles and was a skilled leader in battle.

It had been obvious that there would be rivals for the throne after Edward's death, but as he lay dying, the old king chose Harold Godwineson, the Earl of Wessex (his brother-in-law), as heir. On January 5, 1066, Edward was buried at Westminster Abbey. Later, on the same day, Harold was crowned, after having been confirmed as king by the Witan, a powerful group of nobles who gathered two or three times a year to advise the king.

Although Harold did not have royal Saxon blood in his veins, he was the son of a Scandinavian princess. More important, he was a man with great strength of character. He had proved himself as a military leader in battle against the Welsh, and he was regarded as England's most powerful noble. The Bayeux Tapestry refers to Harold during the time of Edward's reign as Dux Anglorum (Duke of England), and Florence of Worcester called him a *sub regulus* (royal deputy). Clearly, he was held in high regard before he was crowned.

As such, it was no surprise that two of England's other earls (who were brothers), Edwin of Mercia and Morcar of Northumbria, accepted Harold as their king. After all, Harold was married to their sister, the widow of Gruffydd, former king of Wales. Nevertheless, in the history of England, Harold is the only commoner to have been crowned king. And he was to become the only king to die defending his kingdom against foreign invaders.

Harold was crowned in January 1066. During the few months of his reign—before his death at the Battle of Hastings—Harold showed considerable leadership and military skill. This detail from the Bayeux Tapestry reminded people that Harold had been crowned by Stigand, the archbishop of Canterbury. Because Stigand had been excommunicated by the pope, this Norman source implies that Harold's coronation was not legitimate.

RIVAL CLAIMS TO THE THRONE

After his coronation, Harold was concerned that there were rivals who would challenge his claim to the throne. On April 24, 1066, a bright comet, described in *The Anglo-Saxon Chronicle* as a "long-haired star," appeared in the night sky. This is illustrated on the Bayeux Tapestry above a scene showing Harold on his throne shortly after his coronation. Underneath are the ghostly outlines of ships indicating that Harold anticipated an invasion from abroad. The chronicle suggests that the people of England also interpreted the comet as a bad omen. It is now known that this comet reappears in the night sky about every seventy-five years; it has since been named Halley's comet.

For most of Edward's reign, Harold had been a loyal subject, but if he developed any thoughts of succeeding the throne, then it may have been in 1057. That year saw the deaths of two nobles, both with legitimate claims to succeed Edward. They were Ralph, Earl of Hereford, Edward's nephew, and Edward Aetheling, son of Edmund Ironside (king for only a few months in 1016). By 1066, Harold's only rival for the throne in England was Edgar Aetheling, Edward's younger brother. However, as Edgar was only a boy, he was no real threat.

A greater threat was posed by King Harold Hardrada of Norway, who claimed that the English throne had been promised to his father King Magnus by Edward's predecessor, King Hardecanute. Hardrada was supported in his quest for the crown by the Scottish king and by Harold's brother Tostig. Tostig had been Earl of Northumbria but had been stripped of his title by Edward. As a result, he wanted revenge against Harold, who had not supported him.

William's claim to the English throne was even more complicated. First, in terms of bloodline, although William was illegitimate, he was nevertheless the great-nephew of Queen Emma, the mother of Edward the Confessor. Second and more important, William asserted that in 1051 he had been promised the crown by Edward himself.

Edward had been brought up in Normandy, and Edward and William had been friends. Third, William claimed that Harold had sworn to support his right to the throne when he visited Normandy in 1064. In accepting the crown, Harold had broken a solemn oath. The Bayeux Tapestry shows that this oath was taken upon the sacred bones of two English saints that were kept in reliquary boxes.

Why did Harold visit Normandy, and did he really swear to support William? According to the opening scene of the tapestry, Edward sent Harold on a mission without any real explanation as to its aim. After landing in Normandy, Harold is shown being captured by Count Guy of Ponthieu. Afterward, he is taken to meet William. Harold is well looked after and even accompanies William on

Harold *(right)* was compelled or persuaded by Duke William *(left)* to swear an oath that he would support William's claim to the English throne. The oath was sworn with Harold laying his hands on reliquary boxes, probably in Bayeux.

a military campaign in Brittany, which is located to the west of Normandy.

There, he was knighted after having rescued two Normans stuck in quicksand. Whether William regarded Harold as a guest or a prisoner is unclear. Of course, the story depicted on the tapestry supports the Norman perspective. It implies that Edward sent Harold to confirm the offer he made to William for the English throne all those years earlier in 1051.

If Edward did not send Harold to William to confirm his offer of the throne, why did Harold sail to Normandy? William of Jumièges (a Norman monk who wrote an account of William's life in the 1070s) records that Harold returned to England, having obtained the release of his nephew, Hakon, whom William had kept as a prisoner since 1051. But William did not release Harold's own brother, Wulfnoth, whom he also held prisoner.

Was he held as a hostage to make sure Harold kept his oath? Whatever the truth behind the matter, there is no doubt that if Harold did swear to support William under pressure, he later felt little obligation to keep his promise.

WILLIAM SEIZES HIS CHANCE AND PLANS HIS INVASION

The news that Harold had been crowned king in early January 1066 sent William into a rage. In fact, William of Poitiers, his chaplain (personal priest), reported that William felt personally insulted and swore to take revenge by force.

Immediately, William consulted his two half brothers, Odo, bishop of Bayeux, and Robert de Mortain (both legitimate sons from his mother's marriage to Herluin Vicomte de Conteville). He then called his nobles together and asked them to support an invasion of England. William knew that the nobles were expected to supply armed troops whenever he called upon them to take part in military action. However, he was proposing an expedition overseas to confront an enemy of unknown strength and numbers. A large army would need to be gathered, and William felt let down when his nobles refused to support him.

Nonetheless, William remained determined. Using all his diplomatic skills and cunning, he sent an envoy to Pope Alexander II asking for his blessing for an invasion. The pope was a former pupil of William's friend Lanfranc, prior of Bec. Lanfranc persuaded the pope that William was morally in the right to launch what amounted almost to a crusade, in other words, a war justified by religion.

After all, Harold had broken a sacred oath and had been unlawfully crowned by Stigand, who had been excommunicated by five successive popes. And this was despite holding the position of archbishop of Canterbury.

At the same time, William approached each of his nobles individually and promised them land in England in return for their support. This certainly changed their minds. Armed with the pope's approval

This scene from the Bayeux Tapestry shows large numbers of men and horses that were being transported by boat across the *Mare* (sea) separating England from Normandy.

for his mission, William enlisted more troops from other areas of France, as well as other countries in Europe.

Having gathered his troops, large numbers of ships were required to transport men, horses, and supplies across the English Channel. In total, about 500 boats were needed. According to the Bayeux Tapestry, many traditional Viking longboats were hurriedly built at various ports along the north coast of Normandy.

William's own boat was commissioned by his wife, Matilda. Built at Barfleur, it was called the *Mora*. On its prow, the *Mora* had a figurehead of William and Matilda's ten-year-old son, Rufus. He was shown holding a trumpet in one hand and a bow and arrow in the other, with which he is pointing toward England. Matilda firmly supported her husband's plans, especially as she was a descendant of King Alfred the Great of England.

By mid-August, the fleet was assembled at the mouth of the river Dives, located east of Caen in Normandy. Weapons, heavy suits of chain mail carried on poles, newly made arrows, and horses were brought to the coast ready to be loaded. Barrels of wine and sacks of flour (to be used for making bread) were also gathered to feed the army when it arrived in England. There were even three prefabricated wooden stockades, rather like small castles, that could be quickly put together with pegs.

Later, in mid-September, William gave orders for the fleet to sail up the coast to St. Valéry, where the crossing to England would be quicker. All that was needed was a favorable wind blowing from the south to carry them across the narrow channel. As they waited, it seemed to be fate that *Mora*, the name of William's boat, meant "delay." At last their prayers were answered, and the wind changed direction. A trumpet was sounded, and the fleet set sail at about midnight on September 27, 1066. William hoisted the special flag that the pope had sent him. With its cross, the flag was a symbol to William's men that their mission was ordained by God.

WILLIAM CONQUERS ENGLAND

1
2
4
5
6

CHAPTER 3

Sometime after dawn on September 28, William's fleet arrived at the south coast of England and entered a sheltered bay at Pevensey. Before disembarking, scouts were sent out to establish whether the Normans were likely to meet any serious local resistance. When none was met, the masts were lowered and the horses were brought ashore.

William leapt into the sea, but as he waded through the waves and onto the beach, he stumbled and fell. William of Malmesbury, a Saxon historian, noted that his men would have taken this as a sign of bad luck at the start of the invasion. However, seeing William clutching a fistful of sand from the beach, one quick-thinking soldier restored everyone's confidence by shouting out, "You hold England, O future King!"

This scene from the Bayeux Tapestry shows the Normans enjoying a feast before the Battle of Hastings. William's half brother, Bishop Odo *(third from right)*, is shown blessing the food. On the left, some of the Normans are using their shields as tables.

PREPARING FOR BATTLE

Within the ruined walls of the old Roman fort at Pevensey, a prefabricated wooden castle was put up by William's army. This gave them additional protection. But the next day, William moved his base to Hastings, where the other two forts were built. Hastings was a more defensible site, as it was near roads that ran north to London, as well as east and west. From Hastings, he could make an easy retreat to the sea if it became absolutely necessary.

Meanwhile, Norman soldiers were sent into the surrounding countryside to find food. The Bayeux Tapestry depicts cattle being killed and a great feast being prepared, in which Bishop Odo is shown blessing the food.

William knew from his spies that Harold was expecting his invasion. Throughout much of the summer, Harold's army of volunteers had been assembled and was ready to defend England from invasion. It was called the Fyrd and numbered at about 10,000. The men of the Fyrd were obliged to give their service for a two-month period each year. However, on September 8, they had been sent home to collect their harvest, so William probably knew from his spies that the timing of his invasion was to his advantage. In addition, Harold's fleet, which had been stationed off the south coast, had been moved closer to London. What William did not know when he landed was that Harold had reassembled both the Fyrd and his personal bodyguard known as the Housecarls (numbering about 3,000). However, Harold had marched north to meet another invading force that had arrived from Norway.

In mid-September, King Harold heard of Hardrada's invasion and immediately gathered an army ready to march north. Harold was hoping that on his way he would be joined by troops. With amazing drive and determination, his army covered the journey of 180 miles (290 kilometers) in just five

THE KING OF NORWAY INVADES ENGLAND

Hardrada, king of Norway, was a rival for the crown of England. He had been joined by Tostig, the former Earl of Northumbria and Harold's brother. Together, they led a large fleet of Viking longboats up the river Ouse toward the city of York. At Fulford, just south of York, they were met by Edwin of Mercia and Morcar of Northumbria. Both were loyal supporters of Harold's. After a fierce battle, on September 20, 1066, the English were beaten and fled. Hardrada took control of York, whose inhabitants promised to support Hardrada's claim to the English crown. This was not altogether surprising, because for much of its history, York had been a large Viking settlement.

days. They traveled on roads that had been built by the Romans hundreds of years earlier.

On the morning of September 25, Harold took the Viking army by surprise at Stamford Bridge, just northwest of York. During the battle, both Hardrada and Tostig were killed, along with as many as 5,000 members of their army. Harold lost about 2,000 men. After his victory, he generously allowed the remaining Norwegian army to return home in their longboats.

THE BATTLE OF HASTINGS

It is uncertain exactly when Harold heard the news that William had landed. What is clear is that, when news did reach him, he traveled south as fast as possible, reaching London by October 6. Meanwhile, Norman troops were destroying the farmland around Hastings. They were also burning houses and evicting inhabitants.

It was clearly William's plan to make Harold hurry south to defend his people and country and to deny the Saxons time to recover after the battle at Stamford Bridge. Harold had only five days in London before he led his exhausted army south again, toward Hastings. Word was put out that other Fyrdmen were to meet at a place *The Anglo-Saxon Chronicle* describes as the "hoary apple tree." This old gray tree must have been a familiar landmark, and it was here that Harold camped on October 13.

Both sides had scouts watching the enemy, but it must have been difficult to guess what the other side intended to do. Men continued to arrive at the Saxon camp throughout the night. According to a

As depicted in the Bayeux Tapestry, Normans are carrying their heavy chain-mail coats, helmets, and swords on board their boats. At the top right, a man is shown carrying a barrel, which is probably full of wine.

THE NORMAN ARMY

The size of the Norman army probably numbered about 7,000 men. It consisted of about 2,000 cavalrymen, 3,000 infantrymen, and 800 archers. There would also have been more than 1,000 sailors, stable boys, and supply and maintenance staff. Many of these men would have fought in the battle as additional infantrymen.

The Norman knights wore chain-mail coats called hauberks, which were made from interlocking metal rings. They had sleeves to the elbows and came down to about the knees. They split at the front and back to allow freedom of movement on horseback. Some hauberks had hoods, which came up over the head for added protection. A padded undergarment was also worn.

In addition, knights had cone-shaped helmets, fitted with a nose guard. They carried kite-shaped shields made of wood and covered with leather. Their weapons consisted of a lance and a broad-bladed sword, which was more suited to slashing than thrusting. Stirrups, which were not used in England at the time, gave the Norman knights stability on horseback, allowing them to use their weapons more effectively. The Norman infantrymen also had helmets and carried a shield and spear. Many wore hauberks, but some would only have had a leather jacket, which gave little protection. The archers used short bows measuring about 4 feet (1.2 m) in length.

French source, there was heavy drinking. Another source claims that, in contrast, the Normans spent the night at prayer. William of Poitiers records that the duke took Holy Communion at dawn and then addressed his troops, telling them that they were fighting not only for victory but also for their survival.

As they marched toward the Saxons, the French force was divided into three groups. First, there were the Bretons, led by Count Brian of Brittany. Then came the Franco-Flemish, who were commanded by Eustace of Boulogne. Finally, the main body of Normans, who were under the direct command of William, marched out. William rode on a magnificent black horse that had been given to him as a present by King Alfonso of Spain when William had visited Santiago de Compostela on a pilgrimage.

THE SAXON ARMY

The Saxon army consisted of two types of troops. First, there were the king's Housecarls, a highly trained bodyguard of about 3,000 men (although after the Stamford Bridge attack, they probably numbered about 2,000). Each of Harold's two brothers also brought 1,000 Housecarls. Along with these 4,000 men, there

was the part-time Fyrd, which probably numbered about 4,000.

The Bayeux Tapestry shows that the Saxons were well equipped with hauberks and helmets. Some of Harold's troops would have benefited from armor taken from the enemy at Stamford Bridge. Although the Saxons had swords and spears that were similar in design to the Norman weapons, the favored weapon of the Housecarls was the axe.

An axe had a broad blade about 1 foot (0.3 m) wide with a shaft about 3 feet (0.9 m) long. An axe was capable of hacking limbs off with a single blow when swung with force.

A Bayeux Tapestry image showing the Saxon Housecarls beating off a Norman attack at the Battle of Hastings.

The French grouped at Blackhorse Hill in order to put on their hauberks, which had been slung over their horses during the march. Around his neck, William hung the relics upon which Harold had sworn his oath.

Meanwhile, Harold positioned his troops on a long ridge called Senlac Hill. This gave him the advantage of height. Seven or eight rows of about 1,000 men stood shoulder to shoulder behind a shield wall. It would have been a terrifying sight for the Normans, who lined up opposite them on the lower ridge. Between the two armies was a small stream that the Saxons may have dammed in order to make the ground difficult for the Normans to cross.

At about 9 AM on October 14, the French advanced forward until their archers came within firing range of the Saxons. The Saxons were standing behind a wall of interlocking shields. However, the Norman arrows had little impact. As the tapestry shows, the arrows stuck in the Saxon shields, with the soldiers behind standing firm. Next, the French infantry and cavalry attacked. They expected to find that the shower of arrows had weakened the Saxon ranks. Keeping their formation must have been difficult as they struggled up the hill. As they approached the top, the Saxons hurled spears, axes,

This Bayeux Tapestry image shows William organizing his troops before the Battle of Hastings. In medieval times, it was usual for kings to lead their forces into battle. The death of a king might decide the outcome of the battle.

and stones. French knights were thrown off their injured horses. After a bloody struggle, the French force retreated back down the hill.

At this point, members of the Fyrd on Harold's right flank disobeyed his orders. Leaving their ranks, they started to chase the fleeing Breton soldiers down the hill. Directing his men from the rear, William saw what was happening and sent cavalrymen across to cut down the Saxons as they reached the bottom of the slope. Although the Saxons found a small hill from which to defend themselves, they were cut off from the bulk of their army and were all slaughtered. Meanwhile, Bishop Odo gathered the Norman knights together and continued the attack. In the tapestry, Bishop Odo is shown holding a mace (a metal-headed club), because priests were traditionally forbidden from carrying weapons that could shed blood. However, it seems that battering an enemy to death was acceptable!

The most dangerous moment for the French occurred when false news spread that William had been killed. He may well have been thrown from his horse, but the tapestry shows him in his saddle, lifting his helmet to show his face and reassure his troops that he was fine.

Nevertheless, had Harold taken advantage of the panic within the French army and left his hill-top position to mount a full attack, it is possible that he might have achieved victory. As it was, William went on to boost the morale of his troops by fighting bravely in the thick of the battle. There were several more attempts to draw the Saxons out of line using false retreats, but the Saxons continued to stand firm.

A number of lulls in the fighting occurred during the day. These allowed both sides to recover

The death of Harold is shown in this detail from the Bayeux Tapestry. His death, and that of his brothers, was very important for William. If Harold had survived the battle and had not been captured, then it would have been much more difficult for the Normans to impose control on England.

and regroup. After one such pause toward evening, William tried a new tactic. Archers with full quivers of arrows were sent forward to shoot high in the air, dropping their arrows onto the Saxons from above. (These archers are shown in the lower border of the tapestry.) Then, after a further charge and more hand-to-hand combat, came the decisive moment. Harold was killed. At this point, the Saxons started to lose heart, and many less experienced soldiers fled for their lives. The battle had turned in William's favor.

There is some debate as to exactly how Harold died. On the tapestry (the image shown on page 55), the Latin words *Hic Harold Rex Interfectus Est* (Here King Harold was killed) are shown above two people being killed, one with an arrow in his eye and one being hacked to death by a knight on horseback. It is possible that Harold was first struck by an arrow and then finished off by a sword blow. There is a source written by Bishop Guy of Amiens that names four knights who claimed to have killed the king.

After Harold's death, William was with a detachment of knights who chased the remaining Saxons from the battlefield. When he returned, William of Poitiers records that Duke William was obviously moved by the sight of so many dead and injured knights and soldiers on the battlefield. In total, about 4,000 men and perhaps 600 or 700 horses were killed. Stripping the dead of their weapons and hauberks began during the thick of the fighting. The French continued this the next day. The French buried their dead, and William allowed the relatives of Saxons who had died to collect their bodies.

Harold's body was so mutilated that it could not be identified for certain. It was left to Harold's long-term mistress, Edith Swan-Neck, to confirm that the correct corpse had been found. She recognized the body from certain marks that only she would know. Harold was buried under a simple pile of stones on a cliff near Hastings. It was not until years later that he was given a proper burial in the abbey he had founded at Waltham, near London. Meanwhile, William noted the spot where Harold had fallen. The conqueror had sworn that this would be where he would found an abbey if he was victorious.

William Secures His Kingdom

1
2
3
5
6

CHAPTER 4

After the battle, William had hoped that along with the Earls of Mercia and Northumbria, other leading noblemen of England would offer him their submission. As well, he hoped that they would recognize him as their rightful king. But this did not happen. Instead, the earls met in London with other members of the Witan and leading churchmen to discuss the situation.

After debating whether young Prince Edgar should be crowned, they were not able to come to a decision. Meanwhile, at Hastings, William realized it might take some time and possibly further fighting before he would be in control of the country.

William knew he would have to capture London. However, first, he moved east along the coast toward Romney. He intended to punish the town's inhabitants with random killings

Soldiers of the Saxon army are shown on the Bayeux Tapestry. They are fighting on foot while standing behind a wall of shields.

because they had attacked the crews of two Norman ships that had been blown off course during the crossing. William's policy was to use violence to terrorize the English into surrendering.

As a consequence, when his army arrived at the important port of Dover, the Saxons in the fortress surrendered without offering any fight. Norman soldiers started to burn down the fortress. However, its inhabitants had not shown any resistance. Because of this, William, demonstrating his sense of justice, disciplined his troops and compensated the town for its losses.

Next, he marched on to the cathedral city of Canterbury, which surrendered before he arrived. It was here that William became sick and had to stop for a month to recover. Nonetheless, he continued to issue orders. He secured domination of the south of England by sending a party to the city of Winchester. Once there, the party demanded the surrender of the city from Edith, the wife of Edward the Confessor. Edith was also Harold's sister. England's treasure was kept in Winchester.

Once he recovered, William moved toward London, where he aimed to be crowned king. As he approached the capital, the people of Southwark (south London) put up fierce resistance as they defended the only bridge that crossed the river Thames. William therefore moved southwest and then north, making a huge loop.

Carrying out William's policy of creating fear and panic as it encircled London, his army destroyed the countryside and towns it moved through. Finally, at Berkhamsted, just north of London, William was met by Prince Edgar, the Earls of Mercia and Northumbria, and the archbishop of York. They offered the surrender of the country. About this event, *The Anglo-Saxon Chronicle* states, "They gave him hostages and swore oaths of fealty [loyalty], and he promised to be a gracious lord to them."

WILLIAM'S CORONATION

William's coronation, on December 25, 1066, took place in Westminster Abbey, where King Edward the Confessor had been buried less than a year before. The day was chosen partly because William believed that he had conquered England by the will of God and partly, perhaps, because he hoped the English would be too occupied celebrating the Christian feast day to be thinking about causing a riot. As many Saxon noblemen as possible were brought from where they lived to attend the ceremony.

As William was being crowned, the congregation was asked to shout its acceptance of William as king. When the noise inside the abbey was heard by the Norman soldiers on guard outside, they panicked, thinking that the new king had been attacked, and they started to burn down nearby houses.

THE SAXONS REBEL

William returned to Normandy in March 1067. He left two nobles in charge of his kingdom as

William's coronation took place in Westminster Abbey on the banks of the river Thames in London. The coronation of kings was an elaborate ritual symbolizing that the king was chosen by God to be the ruler of the country.

regents. Bishop Odo became Duke of Kent and was given the south of England to look after. William's cousin, William fitz Osbern, who was his most trusted steward, became the Earl of Hereford. He was given the north of England to control. Both regents were supplied with armies, as the Saxons were not expected to accept Norman rule without rebellion. Accompanying William to Normandy were Prince Edgar; Morcar, Earl of Northumbria; Edwin, Earl of Mercia; Stigand; and the archbishop of Canterbury, along with other nobles. Although they were treated as guests, they were really being held as hostages. They could be killed if the Saxons started a rebellion against their new Norman rulers.

Both Odo and the Earl of Hereford (William fitz Osbern) supervised the building of castles throughout the country in order to provide protection for themselves and to demonstrate Norman power. According to *The Anglo-Saxon Chronicle*, they acted like tyrants. They oppressed the Saxons and allowed their troops to treat them badly. Rape and looting were common.

The first serious rebellion took place in Kent, where Odo was responsible for protecting the port of Dover. When Odo was away from the area, the

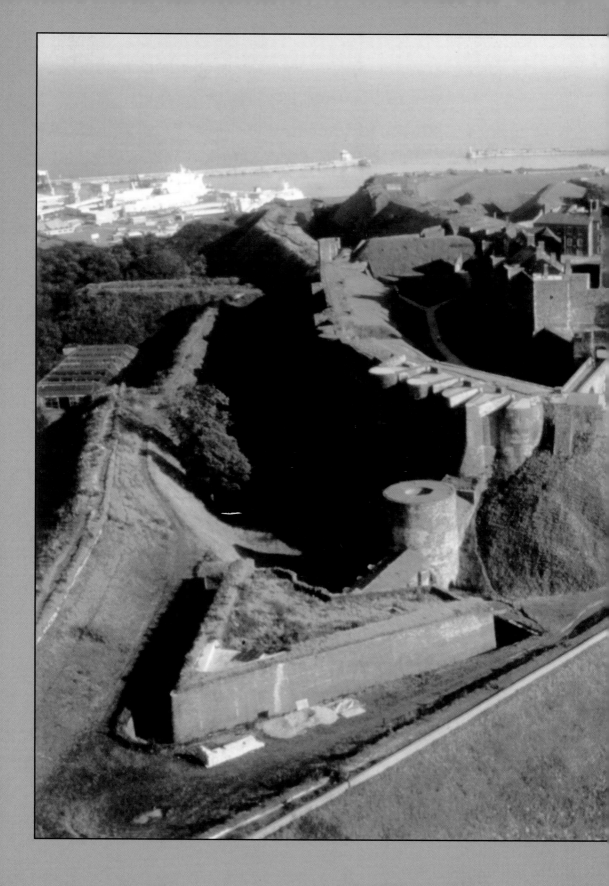

This is an image of Dover Castle. After the Battle of Hastings, William marched to Dover, where the Saxons who guarded the castle surrendered without a fight.

local men of Kent made an unsuccessful attack on Dover Castle. Then news reached William that the people of Northumbria had asked King Swein of Denmark for help. Accordingly, William returned to England in December 1067. He was ready to deal with any invasion. As soon as William arrived, he led an army southwest to lay siege to Exeter, where Harold's mother and her illegitimate sons were the focus of a local uprising. After ordering a castle to be built there, he moved on to Bristol and Gloucester to bring the west of England to order.

At this point, William seemed intent on creating a new Anglo-Norman society in which Saxons and the French would work together. Many of the Saxon nobles were allowed to keep their titles and lands as long as they swore loyalty to William. Those Saxons who had been held in Normandy were released. The south of England was now more firmly under Norman control. After having spent Christmas in the old Saxon capital of Winchester, William gave orders for his wife, Matilda, to be brought to England. Then she was crowned queen in Winchester Cathedral.

Meanwhile, the north of England proved more difficult to control. William had chosen a Norman called Robert of Commines to be Earl of Northumbria.

However, in 1069, a local uprising at Durham ended with Robert being burned to death, along with 900 of his men. The Norman commander at York (a little further south) was also killed. Although William acted quickly, marching north at great speed to take the rebels by surprise, this was the start of another period of rebellion throughout the country.

Matters came to a head when, as William had feared, a Danish fleet landed on the east coast. Local men joined the invasion, and York was taken in September 1069, before the Danes started to move south into Lincolnshire.

William acted with devastating consequences. Marching north, he reclaimed York and then set up a military campaign, moving throughout the north of England to attack the Danes with astonishing deter-mination and energy. Eventually, William agreed to a peace treaty with King Swein. This allowed the Danes to keep the loot they had stolen in return for their promise to leave the country. Meanwhile, Prince Edgar, whom the Saxons still hoped would lead them against the Normans, fled to Scotland. Earl Morcar was taken prisoner again, and Earl Edwin was killed by his own followers.

In revenge, William ordered that huge areas of countryside in the north of England be destroyed.

This scene from the Bayeux Tapestry shows a mother and child fleeing from their home as the Normans set it on fire. Resistance to Norman rule in northern England led William to carry out widespread killings along with the devastation of homes.

This became known as the "harrying of the north" (the word "harried" means "destroyed" or "laid to waste"). The aim of this was to inflict a lesson upon the north that would also be felt throughout the country. Crops were burned, cattle were slaughtered, and even farming equipment was destroyed. As a result, Ordericus Vitalis, a monk writing in the twelfth century, reported that more than 100,000 innocent men, women, and children died of starvation.

The last rebellion William faced was led by Hereward the Wake in 1071. Hereward was regarded as a hero by the Saxons. As his nickname suggests, he was always awake and ready for any danger, especially as he gathered rebels together in the Fens near Ely. The Fens were flat, wet marshlands with small areas of higher ground like islands. This landscape provided Hereward and his men with security from anyone who tried to track them. Eventually, monks from the abbey at Ely showed the Normans a secret path across the Fens to Hereward's camp. Hereward escaped, but most of his followers were captured and killed. The fate of Hereward remains unknown.

THE FEUDAL SYSTEM

William had promised to reward the Norman nobles who fought for him at Hastings by giving them land and making them tenants in chief. In return for the gift of land, William demanded to be paid homage and to be given military service. This became known as the feudal system (from the Latin word *feudum,* meaning "land held").

When granted land, each noble knelt before King William and said, "I promise to become your man, to hold these lands faithfully and perform my due service." The king then told his nobles how many knights they were expected to bring with them when he called upon them for military service. Bishops were also granted land, and they, too, had to provide a certain number of knights when asked.

The number of knights each noble was expected to provide varied according to the amount of land he governed. Some nobles kept the knights they commanded in the castles they built. Other nobles granted their knights their own estates of land called manors. These knights were known as under-tenants and were expected to swear homage to their local lord. However, William made sure all knights first swore allegiance to himself as king. He did not want to face rebellion from his tenants in chief. At the bottom of the feudal ladder, the peasants in each village were expected to serve the knight who was their local lord.

One result of the Saxon rebellions was that more and more land was taken from the Saxons and given to the Normans. Toward the end of William's reign, there were almost no Saxon nobles of any importance. In 1086, William summoned his nobles to Old Sarum Castle at Salisbury, where he made all 170 tenants in chief swear again to be faithful to him. This became known as the Oath of Salisbury.

NORMAN CASTLES

Castles played a very important role in the Norman conquest of England. As well as being designed to provide safety and maximum defense for the people who lived in them, they were also bases from which attacks might be launched. Before the Norman invasion, there had been virtually no castles in England. But by the end of the eleventh century, there were almost 100. As William moved around his kingdom, he personally supervised where castles should be built. Important towns and ports, such as Dover and Cardiff, were protected by castles, as were river crossings, such as at Nottingham and Newcastle. Areas where there was ongoing rebellion or fear of invasion, such as on the Welsh border, became encircled by castles. This way, Norman soldiers were nearby if there was trouble. Perhaps the finest Norman castle built during William's reign is the White Tower. This is the central keep of the Tower of London.

The structure of Norman castles is called a motte and bailey. First, an earth mound called a motte was made. On top of the motte, a small wooden tower, or keep, was built, protected by a

wall of wooden stakes. Around the motte was another wall of stakes enclosing an area called the bailey. In the bailey were living quarters and storerooms. A ditch surrounded the whole site.

Gradually, motte and bailey castles were replaced by much stronger stone castles, which were less vulnerable to fire. The weight of the enormous stone keeps meant that they could not be built on an artificial mound; thus, castles were often built on natural rocky hills. When this was not possible, extra protection, such as a moat filled with water, would have been provided.

Over the next 300 years, castle design became more and more ingenious. The entrance was always a weak spot and more likely to be attacked. Accordingly, the approach would be protected by a drawbridge. A portcullis, which was a sliding wooden and metal gate, could be lowered over the entrance itself for extra protection. The tops of castle walls were given crenellations or battlements, which would protect archers firing arrows

The White Tower of the Tower of London was built by William to help control his capital city. At first, a wooden fort was erected on the site, but in 1078, this was replaced by the current stone keep, which stands 90 feet (27 meters) high.

on the enemy below. Machicolations (ledges) were built that jutted out from battlements. These allowed defenders to drop rocks on enemy soldiers or fend off siege ladders. When viewed from the outside, windows looked like narrow slits. But from the inside, they widened sharply, which allowed archers to fire in all directions. If attackers did manage to scale the outer walls of a castle, they would have little hope of getting any farther.

CHURCH AND STATE

1
2
3
4

CHAPTER 5

6

In contrast to the ruthlessness that William showed as a military commander, he was a committed Christian. As king of England, he took an active interest in church matters. As *The Anglo-Saxon Chronicle* states, "Though stern beyond measure to those who opposed his will, he was kind to those good men who loved God."

WILLIAM AND THE CHURCH

As Duke of Normandy, William reserved the right to appoint the archbishop of Rouen, along with all other bishops and abbots of monasteries. Many of the men he appointed were friends and relatives whom he could trust as advisers and administrators. During the Middle Ages, few people could read and write in Latin, the language used for important correspondence and legal documents. However, all rulers knew that educated and respected church leaders were useful administrators. A bishop could also be a powerful political supporter with great influence over the people in his diocese (the area for which he was responsible).

After the conquest of England, William appointed his friend Lanfranc to be archbishop of Canterbury. Lanfranc was an Italian monk who had previously helped William gain the pope's approval for his marriage to Matilda. In recognition for this service, William had promoted him to abbot of the St. Étienne abbey in Caen.

When Lanfranc was later appointed archbishop of Canterbury, he made sure that he was acknowledged as the most influential church leader in England. This was important because, at the time, there were two archbishops in England. There was an archbishop of York and an archbishop of Canterbury, and both were of equal importance. William wanted to reorganize the church in England, and he chose Lanfranc to carry out a program of reforms. Lanfranc argued that he was the most important church leader in England because Christianity had first been established at Canterbury.

BISHOPS AND ABBEYS

The most obvious change to the church in England after 1066 was that Normans, rather than Saxons, were appointed as bishops. By the end of William's reign in 1087, there were only two Saxon bishops remaining. In addition, to emphasize the importance of the role of the bishops, new Norman-style cathedrals were built, and other earlier Saxon cathedrals were rebuilt.

Other reforms were decided upon at church councils held in 1072, 1075, and 1076. Bishops would be given assistants called archdeacons to help them undertake their work. All priests and bishops had to be unmarried and remain celibate. Any priest accused of an offense was to be tried in church court, rather than an ordinary one. William clearly wanted to encourage a sense of morality within the church, especially at a time when bribes were sometimes given as church posts were filled. This was something that William would not tolerate.

William also included bishops in the feudal system. Many cathedrals owned large areas of the countryside and were able to raise taxes from the peasants who farmed the land. In addition, bishops sometimes received money from benefactors.

When a noble was dying, he might ask a bishop to bury him in the cathedral and pray for his soul after death. In return for this service, the cathedral might receive a large sum of money. As a consequence of this wealth, bishops were expected to supply the king with knights for military duty when required. For example, the bishop of Winchester was obliged to maintain sixty fully armed knights. Bishops were also expected to administer justice at law courts and help maintain peace. At Durham, in the north of England, a great Norman cathedral was built beside a castle on a rocky hill overlooking a bend in the river Wear.

The bishop of Durham was given considerable responsibility for governing the extreme north of the country. Even at present, Durham County is still known as the Land of the Prince Bishops.

Abbeys also flourished under William's rule. The work of monks (who lived in abbeys and monasteries) during the Middle Ages contributed greatly to society. They kept records, such as *The Anglo-Saxon Chronicle*, and they sometimes taught local boys to read and write. They also helped cure the sick and were good at farming. Both William and Matilda started several abbeys in Normandy. William also encouraged the growth of monasteries in his new kingdom.

The Great Domesday Book records details of the survey of England that William ordered to be carried out during 1086. It was written on parchment, which is made from specially prepared animal skin.

THE GREAT DOMESDAY BOOK

William celebrated Christmas in 1085 at Gloucester. During this time, he spent many hours consulting his leading advisers and nobles. He decided to order a detailed survey of England to be carried out during the following year. Part of the reason for the survey was to enable William to work out how much tax could be raised within his kingdom.

Seven teams of royal officials summoned land-owners to country courts, and extensively detailed lists were made of who owned an area of land and how much it was worth. In addition, everyone who was summoned was also asked who had owned each area of land before the Norman Conquest, and they were asked how much it had been worth. Cattle, pigs, and even plows, mills, and fishponds were listed.

When all the information had been collected, a summary of the survey was made in Winchester on about 400 pages of parchment paper. Looking carefully at the handwriting, it appears to have been written by one man. Soon, it was referred to as *The Great Domesday Book*. This was because it made one think of the day of judgment after death, when people believed God would judge everyone according to their actions during life.

The Great Domesday Book was an extraordinary achievement because it was so detailed and because it was compiled so quickly. Only a monarch with huge drive and ability to organize could have over-seen such a project. *The Great Domesday Book* consists of two volumes and can be seen at the Records Office in London. It provides a very good picture of what life was like in England during the reign of William and how it had changed following the Norman Conquest.

LIFE IN NORMAN ENGLAND

The overall population in England during William's reign was probably around 2 million. London was the largest city, followed by York and Norwich. But most of the Saxon population lived in small country villages. In addition, there were about 25,000 Normans in the country. This number included soldiers, knights, and nobles.

Farming was the dominant occupation for most Saxon peasants at the bottom of the feudal system. Growing crops was important, as it provided food for people and animals. Beer, the main drink, was made from barley. There were few cows, as most people drank goat's milk. As well, many people kept a few pigs. The pigs, which ate acorns, were allowed to wander in the woodlands surrounding each village.

Peasants were divided into four classes. This was figured out according to how much land a peasant owned and how he paid his taxes to his overlord. An overlord was most likely a knight in charge of a manor. There were free men who each owned a fair amount of land but had to pay their overlord for this privilege. Second, the villeins each owned about thirty acres (twelve hectares)

WILLIAM'S FAVORITE PASTIME

William loved hunting for deer in the vast areas of forest that existed in Normandy and England. He gave orders for the creation of what became called the New Forest. This is located near Winchester, in southern England. Ordericus Vitalis states, "Being a great lover of forests, he [the king] laid waste to more than sixty parishes and substituted beasts of the chase for human beings that he might satisfy his ardour [passion] for hunting."

The local peasants were annoyed that their villages were destroyed. But they were also angry about the new forest laws, which made it illegal for the peasants to hunt in the forests themselves.

and paid rent to their overlords by working for them for free during harvest. They might also be expected to provide their overlord with food from their land. Third, there were cottagers. They each owned a small amount of land and paid their rent by working for their overlords one day a week. On the other days, they would earn some money by working for other better-off peasants such as

This huntsman on horseback is blowing a horn. Two hounds are shown running ahead, chasing a stag (male deer). Hunting remained the sport of kings for hundreds of years.

shepherds, swineherds (people who cared for pigs), or blacksmiths. The last group was the slaves. In 1066, they numbered about 25,000. However, during William's reign, slavery became less common. This was partly because slaves did not earn any money and so could not pay taxes.

Over time, some of the Norman soldiers in England started to marry Saxon girls and settle down.

This helped promote a more lasting peace throughout the country. It also influenced the English language. This was because French vocabulary started to be used alongside traditional Saxon. This was particularly evident with regard to food. The Saxons would refer to cows, deer, chicken, and sheep, whereas the Normans ate the food provided by the peasants but would use the words "beef," "venison" (deer), "poultry," and "mutton" (sheep), which are French in origin.

LATER YEARS

William enjoyed good health throughout his reign, and even though he became increasingly overweight as he grew older, he never lost his energy or commanding presence. The lands he ruled as king of England and Duke of Normandy were vast, and there were always border disputes that demanded his personal attention.

CHAPTER 6

BORDER DISPUTES

After the earlier Saxon rebellions, the Norman hold on England was not in any serious danger. However, William took action to contain both the Welsh and the Scots. The Earls of Hereford, Chester, and Shrewsbury (whom William had appointed) were responsible for preventing Welsh raids in the west of England. But as a further precaution, in 1081, William built an impressive castle

This is an image of the castle at Caen. Its construction started in 1060 and continued during the reign of William's son Henry.

at Cardiff in south Wales. Farther north, the boundary with Scotland remained in dispute for centuries. Meanwhile, King Malcolm III of Scotland was forced to become William's vassal.

A more serious dispute developed in 1076 on the border between western Normandy and Brittany. Ralph de Gael, who was the Earl of Norfolk in eastern England, was involved in a plot to depose William as king. When the plot was discovered, de Gael fled to Brittany, where he was an important landowner. From his castle at Dol on the Normandy border, he sent an appeal to King Philip I of France, asking for his support against William. William immediately laid siege to the castle at Dol. However, he was forced to retreat to Normandy when King Philip arrived with an army. This was William's first defeat in battle in about twenty years.

FAMILY ISSUES

In addition to continuing border disputes, William's family brought him cause for concern during the last years of his life. This was particularly so in 1083, when Matilda died. William had valued his wife's advice and trusted her to rule Normandy when he was away. After her burial in the abbey she had founded in Caen, William swore that he would give up hunting as a token of respect. As far as we know, he kept his pledge.

The king and queen had sons named Robert, Richard, William, and Henry and daughters named Agatha, Adeliza, Cecily, Adela, and Constance. Of all of these children, it was Robert who provided William with the biggest difficulty. He was nick-named Curthose, meaning "short trousers," and was Matilda's favorite son. As a young man, he had been given the title of Count of Maine. He inherited this title through his marriage at the age of eleven

Hand-to-hand combat was a bloodthirsty business—the injuries that could be inflicted were horrific. Knights were trained to fight on foot and on horseback.

to Margaret, sister of Herbert II, Count of Maine. When William became king of England, Robert wanted to become Duke of Normandy. Matilda supported her son to an extent, which only annoyed William. He had fought hard to win both Normandy and England. He was not going to give up any of the land he ruled, even if that meant denying his son.

In 1078, William suffered a defeat when Robert sided with the French king and William's other enemies from Brittany, Maine, and Anjou. Father and son met in battle near Gerberoy, and Robert wounded

William's hand. It took until 1080 until the two men were again on speaking terms.

Of William and Matilda's other children, their second son, Richard, was killed in a riding accident in the New Forest when he was quite young. William, their third son, was nicknamed Rufus because he had a red face. Henry, their fourth son, was judged by William to be the most able. Their eldest daughter, Agatha, died while on her way to marry the king of Castile in Spain. Their second and third daughters, Adeliza and Cecily, both became nuns. Adela, their fourth daughter, married the Count of Blois, and Constance, the youngest, married the Count of Brittany.

Bishop Odo, the Duke of Kent, also caused difficulty. William quarreled with Odo in 1082 and had him arrested when he learned that Odo was planning a trip to Rome in an attempt to put himself forward as the next pope. Odo was a man of enormous greed and selfish ambition. William probably felt that he would be an unsuitable candidate. Odo was imprisoned in the Rouen castle until William died, and then he was released.

WILLIAM'S DEATH AND BURIAL

During July 1087, William, aged about sixty, led an army over the eastern border of Normandy into an area known as the French Vexin. Here, he attacked the town of Mantes. Soldiers from Mantes had been crossing the border and carrying out raids in Normandy. In revenge, William planned to destroy the town. As his soldiers looted buildings and set fire to the town, Ordericus Vitalis writes that the king "fell sick from the excessive heat and his great fatigues [tiring activities]."

It is impossible to be sure exactly what happened, but it is documented that William suffered severe internal injuries. Perhaps his horse had stood on a burning ember and reared up, throwing William heavily onto the metal pommel on the front of his saddle. Ordericus Vitalis also describes the old king as being "very corpulent," or heavily built. Perhaps this made him less agile on horseback than he would have been as a younger man, and this led to a riding accident.

THE END IS NEAR

William was taken back to Rouen, but he was later transferred from the noisy capital to the Priory of St. Gervais. Here, the monks were able to care for him and pray for his recovery. However, soon it became clear that he was dying. William looked back upon his life and confessed that, although he had been born to lead the life of a soldier, he nevertheless regretted the loss of lives he had caused. At the same time, he felt that his conscience was eased a little because he had regarded the English crown as rightfully his. He also took pride in the fact that, throughout his life, he had used his power to help and develop the church.

William died early in the morning on September 9, 1087. Sadly, his servants greedily looted his personal belongings in his room. Rouen was in a state of panic as news of his death spread. The archbishop of Rouen gave orders for William's body to be taken by boat down the river Seine and then over land to Caen. There, it was prepared for burial in St. Étienne, the Abbaye-aux-hommes. This was the monastery founded by William after his marriage to Matilda.

AN UNDIGNIFIED FAREWELL

The funeral service was far from dignified. First, a fire broke out in houses near the abbey as the body was being carried through the city. There was chaos as quite a number of people following the coffin stopped to see what was happening and helped put out the flames. Then, an old man came forward, claiming that the abbey had been built on land he

William's tombstone in the Church of St. Étienne has a simple dignity.

had once owned but had not been paid for. To satisfy the man, William's son Henry gave the man 60 shillings and promised to pay him more later.

Finally, the stone burial tomb was found to be too short. As a result, William's bones were broken as his body was forced inside the tomb.

During the French Revolution in the eighteenth century, the tomb was opened, and William's bones were thrown into the nearby river Orne. Only a thighbone remained, which was reburied under a simple stone slab in front of the altar in 1987.

THE QUESTION OF SUCCESSION

As he lay dying, William was persuaded by the archbishop of Rouen to settle his differences with Robert, his eldest son. He confirmed that Robert would become Duke of Normandy. William would probably have preferred to have left all his lands to just one of his sons so that his inheritance would have remained intact. However, he had not been on good terms with Robert for many years, and William, his third son, was his favorite. Therefore, the conqueror of England left the English throne to William, while his fourth son, Henry, was far from happy when he received only £5,000.

William II proved to be an unpopular king. Like his father, he was often ruthless, but William II lacked diplomacy. When he was killed by an arrow in 1100 while hunting in the New Forest, many people suspected that it was not an accident and that he had been murdered. His younger brother, Henry, had also been in the New Forest. Henry immediately rode to nearby Winchester, where he demanded the keys to the treasury and proclaimed himself king.

By right, the crown should have been passed to Robert, the eldest brother, but in 1096, he had gone on a crusade to the Holy Land, where he was asked to become king of Jerusalem. However, Robert had declined the throne and was on his way back to Normandy. Quickly, he gathered an army to invade England, but when he met Henry, the two brothers hugged each other and patched up their differences.

Sadly, peace between them did not last. When Robert started to cause trouble in Normandy, Henry invaded and captured his brother in 1106 at the Battle of Tinchebray. Robert was imprisoned in Cardiff Castle, where he spent the final twenty-eight years of his life. Henry ended up, like his father, as both Duke of Normandy and king of England.

SUMMING UP WILLIAM THE CONQUEROR: A COMPLEX TASK

William was obviously a born leader, with all the necessary qualities of vision, strength, and determination. But he was also a master of propaganda—the art of portraying oneself in a favorable light. This makes it difficult to have an accurate sense of what he was really like.

He was certainly a man of contrasts. For example, *The Anglo-Saxon Chronicle* records that he created laws and enforced peace in England "so that a man might go the length and breadth [width] of the king-dom with his pockets full of gold . . . and no man durst

Robert, William's eldest son, went on a crusade to Jerusalem. This crusader has a cross sewn on his tunic. The Latin word *crux*, meaning "cross," is the origin of the word "crusade."

slay [kill] another." However, it was only by his ruth-lessness that peace was established in the first place. The destruction he caused in the north of England brought poverty to that area for generations. It can also be said that William was generous to individuals and the church, and yet he was also greedy. He was a supreme opportunist, ready to take advantage of situations for his own benefit. And yet, after the early Saxon rebellions had been dealt with, William rarely visited his kingdom. He perhaps made as few as four visits in the last ten years of his reign.

William's achievements are easier to describe. He conquered a country, ordered castles and cathedrals to be built, and established law and order. And even from this distance in time, the Norman invasion still stirs the imagination. Differences in the various accounts of William's life continue to cause heated debate among historians. What is certain is that the changes brought about by the Norman Conquest are still evident today. England was a very different country after the events of 1066.

TIMELINE

1027–1028	Birth of William.
1035	Death of Duke Robert (William's father). William becomes Duke of Normandy.
1047	William defeats a rebel army at Val-és-Dunes.
1049	Pope Leo IX forbids William to marry his cousin Matilda.
1051	William claims that Edward the Confessor offered him the English crown.
1053	William and Matilda marry.
1054	William defeats the French king at the Battle of Mortemer.
1056	King Henry of France is once again defeated by William.
1059	The pope pardons William for marrying Matilda.
1066	William invades England and defeats Harold.
1067	Revolts in the west of England are subdued.
1069	The north of England is laid to waste following revolts.
1071	The last revolt, led by Hereward the Wake, is crushed.
1076	William suffers a rare defeat while attacking a castle in Brittany.
1078	William is injured by his son Robert in battle in Normandy.
1082	Bishop Odo, William's half brother, is arrested.
1083	The death of Queen Matilda.
1085	William orders *The Great Domesday Book* to be compiled.
1086	The Oath of Salisbury.
1087	Death of King William.

GLOSSARY

abbey A building where monks live.

alliance An agreement between rulers.

ally A country that supports another country in a war.

Angles People from Germany who invaded England during the Dark Ages.

Anglo-Saxon Chronicle, The A record of important events kept by Saxon monks.

archbishop The highest rank of churchman in a country.

archdeacon Churchman who assists an archbishop.

barbarian A term used to describe a member of various eastern European tribes who attacked western Europe in the Dark Ages.

battlements Raised parapets at the top of castle walls, which gave protection against enemy arrows.

Bede A monk who lived from circa 673–735 in northern England. He became known as the Venerable Bede because of his scholarship.

benefactor A person who gives money to a church or a charity.

bishop A clergyman in charge of an area called a diocese.

bloodline People directly related from one generation to the next.

cavalry Soldiers on horseback.

celibate Living a life without engaging in the act of sex.

chain mail A coat made of metal rings, worn for protection in battle.

chastity Not engaging in the act of sex.

comet A body of small particles and gas that moves in a large orbit through space.

commission Payment for something to be made.

commoner Somebody who is not related to the monarch.

count A title given to an important noble.

crenellations Defensive battlements on a castle wall, used to provide shelter for protection, with openings for firing arrows.

crusade A war fought by European soldiers against Muslims who had captured the Holy Land.

cunning   Imaginative planning.

day of judgment   The Christian belief that on the last day of the world, everyone will be judged by God according to his or her actions during life.

depose   To remove a king or queen from power by force.

diocese   The district over which a bishop is in charge.

draught   The depth of water needed to float a boat.

drawbridge   A bridge that can be lowered over a moat or ditch.

duke   A high-ranking noble, possibly related to royalty.

envoy   A person sent on an important diplomatic mission.

excommunicate   To ban somebody from the church.

fealty   Sworn loyalty to a king or noble.

feudal system   A system of land ownership in return for tax.

fleet   A group of boats sailing together.

Fyrd   The volunteer army in Saxon England.

Halley's comet   A bright comet that moves in an orbit around the sun and is visible from Earth every seventy-five years. It is named after the British astronomer Edmond Halley (1656–1742), who was the first to work out the times of its orbit and predict when it would next be seen.

Holy Communion   Part of a church service that involves drinking wine and eating bread in remembrance of Jesus.

hostage   Somebody held captive.

Housecarls   The personal bodyguard of Saxon kings.

illegitimate   Being born to unmarried parents.

infantrymen   Soldiers who fight on foot.

keep   The main building at the center of a castle.

knight   A highly trained soldier in the Middle Ages, who fought on horseback.

Latin   The language originally used by the ancient Romans.

longboat   A wooden boat of Viking design also used by Normans. Longboats had one mast and a single sail. They could also be rowed.

looting   Stealing from damaged buildings during war.

mace   A metal club with a flanged head.

machicolations   Wooden battlements that hang over a castle wall, from which boulders and boiling water might be dropped upon an enemy.

manor   An area of land and village over which a knight would be in charge.

military campaign   A series of battles.

moat   A water-filled ditch surrounding a castle.

monarch   The king or queen of a country.

monastery   A building where monks live.

monk   A man who lives in a monastery and devotes himself to the work and service of God.

noble   A person with a title, such as earl or count, who has inherited or been granted land by the monarch.

Normandy   An area in northwest France, where Vikings settled.

Norsemen   The name given to raiders from the North who attacked areas of Europe.

oath   A promise that, if broken, would bring punishment from God.

omen   A natural event taken as a prediction of the future.

ordained   Ordered or blessed by God.

overlord   A person superior in power and position to another in the feudal system.

parchment   Specially prepared animal skin used instead of paper.

pay homage   To make an oath of loyalty to a superior noble, king, or queen.

penance   A punishment or task, given by the church, to a person who has sinned. By completing the penance, a person indicates that he or she is sorry and the person is granted forgiveness.

pilgrimage   A journey to a place of religious significance.

pommel   The raised part at the front of a saddle.

pope   The leader of the Catholic Church who lives in Rome.

portcullis   The metal or wood lattice door of a castle.

predecessor   Somebody who previously held a title or fulfilled a role.

prior   The head of a monastery.

prow   The front of a boat.

quicksand   Soft sand, into which it is easy to sink.

regent   Someone who governs the country when the king or queen is abroad.

relics   The bones or belongings of a saint.

reliquary box   A box containing the bones of a dead saint.

reprisal   The act of taking violent revenge.

runes   Letters in Viking writing.

Santiago de Compostela   The burial place of St. James the Apostle in northwest Spain.

Saxons   People of German descent living in England at the time of the Norman invasion.

Scandinavia   Northern European countries, including Denmark, Norway, and Sweden, from which the Norsemen originated.

siege   Attack on an enemy castle or town.

steward   A high-ranking servant who managed his lord's land and property.

stirrups   The metal rest or support for the rider's feet while on horseback.

stockade   A wooden fence put up around an army to provide protection.

succession The issue concerning who becomes the next monarch.

surrender To give up fighting and agree to the enemy's wishes.

tanner A person who makes leather from animal skins.

tenant in chief A noble given a large area of land by the king.

undertenant Somebody granted land by a tenant in chief.

vassal Somebody who swears loyalty to an overlord.

villeins Peasants at the bottom of the feudal system.

Welsh The people who live in Wales.

Wessex The historic name for a large area of southern England.

Witan A group of leading nobles who the king consulted on important matters.

FOR MORE INFORMATION

WEB SITES
Due to the changing nature of Internet links, the Rosen Publishing Group, Inc., has developed an online list of Web sites related to the subject of this book. This site is updated regularly. Please use this link to access the list:

http://www.rosenlinks.com/lema/wico

FOR FURTHER READING

Cootes, Richard John. *The Middle Ages.* New York: Longman, 1996.

Gravett, Christopher. *Hastings 1066.* Oxford, England: Osprey Publishing, 2002.

Gravett, Christopher. *Norman Knights.* Oxford, England: Osprey Publishing, 2002.

Heath, Ian. *The Vikings.* Oxford, England: Osprey Publishing, 2002.

Hilliam, David. *Kings, Queens, Bones and Bastards.* Stroud, England: Sutton Publishing, 1998.

Leyser, Henrietta, and Haydn Middleton. *Invasion and Integration.* Oxford, England: Oxford University Press, 1990.

Steele, Philip. *The Medieval World.* London: Kingfisher, 2000.

Stimpson, Ben. *The Medieval World.* Cheltenham, England: Nelson Thornes, 1998.

BIBLIOGRAPHY

Ashley, Maurice. *William I.* London: Book Club Associates, 1973.

Brooke, Christopher. *The Saxon and Norman Kings.* Glasgow, Scotland: Fontana, 1989.

Guest, Ken, and Denise Guest. *British Battles.* London: HarperCollins, 1997.

Jones, John. *The Medieval World.* Walton on Thames, England: Thomas Nelson Ltd., 1979.

Matthew, Donald. *Atlas of Medieval Europe.* Oxford, England: Phaidon Press Ltd, 1983.

Parker, Geoffrey. *Warfare.* Cambridge, England: Cambridge University Press, 2000.

Rud, Morgens. *The Bayeux Tapestry.* Copenhagen, Denmark: Christian Ejlers Publishers, 2002.

Seymour, William. *Battles in Britain.* London: Book Club Associates, 1979.

Wright, Peter Poyntz. *Hastings.* Moreton-in-Marsh, England: The Windrush Press, 1999.

INDEX

ABOUT THE AUTHOR

Paul Hilliam is a graduate of London University. He is Senior Master at Derby Grammar School, in England, where he enjoys teaching history and religious studies. He has traveled throughout Europe, the Middle East, and India visiting sites of historical interest.

CREDITS